The Island

A
Natural
History
of
Vancouver
Island

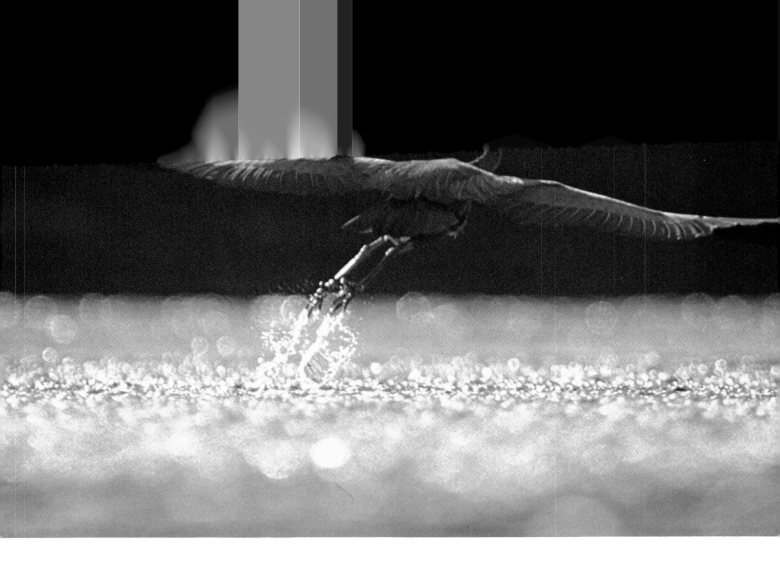

The Island
A Natural History of Vancouver Island

Photographs and text by Tim Fitzharris

Toronto
Oxford University Press
1983

CANADIAN CATALOGUING IN PUBLICATION DATA

Fitzharris, Tim, 1948-
    The Island: a natural history of Vancouver Island

Includes index.
ISBN 0-19-540392-4

1. Natural history — British Columbia — Vancouver
Island.   2. Vancouver Island (B.C.) — Description
and travel.   I. Title.

QH106.2.B7F57   508.711′34   C82-094616-8

© Oxford University Press (Canadian Branch) 1983
OXFORD is a trademark of Oxford University Press
ISBN 0-19-540392-4
1 2 3 4 — 6 5 4 3
Printed in Hong Kong by
EVERBEST PRINTING COMPANY LIMITED

Pacific madrona

To Erma

Acknowledgements

I am indebted to R. Wayne Campbell, Associate Curator of Vertebrate Zoology at the British Columbia Provincial Museum, and all the staff members who helped in reviewing the text and photographs for scientific accuracy; any errors that may remain are entirely my responsibility. In addition, I would like to express my gratitude to Sheryl Fitzharris, for her patient typing of the manuscript; to Bayne Stanley, for his help in supplying Canon photographic equipment; and to the staff at Oxford University Press, especially Roger Boulton and Sally Livingston, for their creative assistance and care in the production of this book.

Great blue heron

Contents

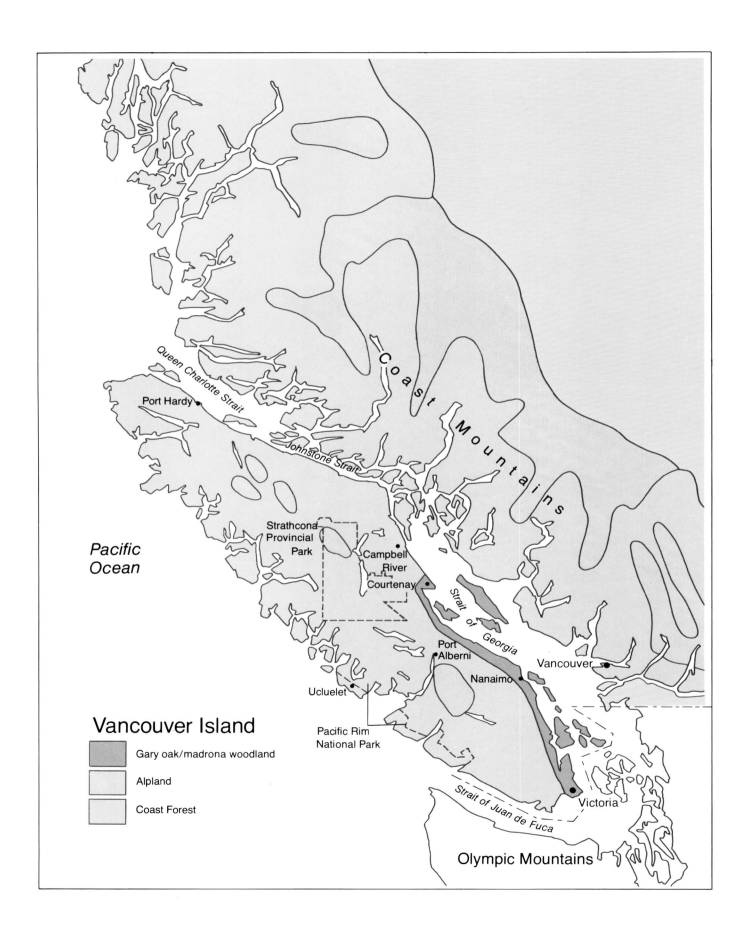

Pacific
Ocean

Queen Charlotte Strait

Port Hardy

Johnstone Strait

Coast Mountains

Strathcona
Provincial
Park

Campbell
River

Courtenay

Strait of Georgia

Port
Alberni

Vancouver

Nanaimo

Ucluelet

Pacific Rim
National Park

Victoria

Strait of Juan de Fuca

Olympic Mountains

Vancouver Island

- Gary oak/madrona woodland
- Alpland
- Coast Forest

Introduction

BIG TRUNCHEON PAWS press gingerly against the sides of a plastic yoghurt container as an agile tongue, pristine pink, flicks at the remnant goop and then retracts. The massive head lifts, and two dull dark eyes gaze over the surrounding ridges of trash. Suddenly my viewfinder goes black — another bear is shuffling by at close range. Dangling from its muzzle are the ripe remains of a hefty meat roast, loose and jiggling in the hot midday sun. A few metres to one side, two younger bears rummage shoulder to shoulder, ploughing at a heap of twisted cardboard, Javex bottles, tin cans, *Time* magazines, neon-green fluff, and other cast-offs. In the distance, I can make out almost a dozen more bears randomly sprawled over the logged hillside, stuffed fat from their summer-long binge. Many carry seeping wounds as a result of quarrelsome close-quarter feeding.

A garbage truck from the nearby Canadian Forces base pulls into the compound and begins to tip its load. Ravens and bald eagles hunkered in the Douglas firs on the crest of the hill watch the procedure keenly. Soon it will be their turn to scavenge among the rusty tricycles and empty Tide boxes.

Shooting at the Holburg dump on northern Vancouver Island was one of the most memorable and provocative experiences I had while working on the photographs for this book. The scene underlines an aspect of the island's natural history that I encountered many times: the disfiguring effect of human activities on the wilderness. Speedboats chasing killer whales up and down Johnstone Strait, a river otter romping on a beach strewn with styrofoam hamburger cartons and beer-bottle shards, and seals dodging floatplanes in Victoria's downtown harbour; deer mauled by neighbourhood dogs, and naturalists doing guard duty over the precious marmot colonies; mining operations in Strathcona Park, and everywhere the broad scars and open wounds made by busy logging companies — these are only a few of the images that tell the story. Not to mention the crowded highways and sprawling suburbs, the factories and transmission lines, and all the other unsavoury by-products of commercial progress emanating from the population centres along the inner coast.

Such flaws are all too evident in an area with unique scenic beauty, an inviting climate, and an exceedingly rich natural history. Clearly,

The bald eagle is a common feature of Vancouver Island's forests and waterways.

Sitka spruce frame a surf-hammered stretch of the outer coastline. ▷

human beings dominate Vancouver Island, consuming more of its resources than all other animals combined, and at a rate that far outstrips the ecosystem's capacity to replenish itself or recover. In this light, it seems particularly valuable to set down a personal record of the island's wildness as it exists in 1983. Certainly it will not be quite the same ten years from now.

To understand the natural history of Vancouver Island, it is essential to become familiar with the region's geography and climate. The largest island on the west coast of North America, Vancouver Island is 450 kilometres long and 130 kilometres across at its widest point. In shape it resembles a lumpy cigar. Nestled

◁ Perched on the snag of a Douglas fir, a bald eagle surveys the mountainous terrain characteristic of the island.

into a protective notch of the continental land mass, it is walled in by the towering mountains of the British Columbia mainland and Washington's Olympic Peninsula. This barrier not only shields the island from extreme continental weather systems, but works to keep the plant and animal communities of the Pacific coast separate from those of the interior regions. Vancouver Island is further insulated from mainland influences by the relatively benign Straits of Juan de Fuca to the south and the island-clogged Straits of Georgia, Johnstone, and Queen Charlotte to the east. The island's northern end and most of the western coast lie open to the pounding waves and sometimes violent weather of the Pacific Ocean.

The outer coastline is a chaotic, convoluted mass of rocky islands, precipitous headlands,

Near a clump of red-tinted madrona trunks on the dry south coast, a river otter takes a momentary breather from its romp in the dirt.

A well-synchronized flock of migrating sandpipers comes to ▷ rest on a pebble beach.

and deep, twisting fiords, some of which penetrate more than half-way across the island. Here road construction is impractical, and the area is sparsely populated. Most of the isolated villages are accessible only by boat, floatplane, or circuitous, low-grade logging road. The inner coast is more hospitable, and a good paved road runs its length, joining the numerous settlements and agricultural areas that lie along this strip of lowland. In general, however, the terrain is mountainous. A jumble of peaks and ranges covers most of the land away from the coast. Few of the island's mountains rise above 2,100 metres, and by mainland standards they are

decidedly puny. Nevertheless, they distinguish the landscape with an aura of rugged wilderness. A number of deep valleys slash randomly through these ranges, some extending across the island to merge with the fiords of the outer coast.

Vancouver Island's land mass and soil are the elemental building blocks of its natural history. It is the effect of climate on this geological matrix that determines the nature of the covering vegetation and the wildlife it supports. The climate can almost be summed up in two words: 'wet' and 'mild'. Although the island's southernmost tip lies some 500 kilometres further north than Toronto, its growing season is the longest in Canada (280 frost-free days at Victoria, as compared with 165 at Toronto, 150 at

◁ *The Vancouver Island marmot is Canada's only endangered endemic mammal species.*

7

The lush beauty of a virgin rain forest.

Halifax, and 92 at Calgary). In the dead of winter, the temperature often reaches a balmy +5 degrees centigrade. Average July temperatures, on the other hand, rarely exceed +15 to +18 degrees (Toronto and Montreal average +21).

The reason for this surprisingly moderate climate is the stabilizing effect of the Pacific Ocean, particularly the Japanese current. Sixty-five hundred kilometres away in the tropics, warm water is driven westward by the trade winds; turning north on encountering the Philippine Islands, it then veers eastward off the Japanese land mass, and prevailing westerly winds carry it across the Pacific to bathe the entire British Columbia coastline in mild temperatures. When the warm Pacific winds collide with Vancouver Island's outer coast, the abundant moisture carried in the air begins to fall as rain. As the air

mass is forced upward by the mountains, it is further cooled, and precipitation increases dramatically. The outer coastal regions record average annual rainfalls in the 250-centimetre range, while mountainous regions further inland may receive twice that amount. Thus, by the time the air crosses the island and descends to the inner straits, it has dried considerably. Annual precipitation in Nanaimo (100 centimetres) and Victoria (65 centimetres) is comparable to the Toronto average (78 centimetres), most of it occurring during fall and winter.

This combination of climate and geography results in a landscape almost totally upholstered in forests, most of them coniferous. Each forest association is custom-designed by local influences such as terrain, micro-climate, soil characteristics, elevation, and past forest-fire occurrences. Four species of large trees are predominant. The Sitka spruce is most common along the coast, usually growing in the fog belts of exposed ocean shores. The renowned Douglas fir flourishes under a fair range of conditions, though even the most spectacular rain-forest stands are not stable, since seedlings of this species are unable to grow in the shade of the parent trees. In contrast, the forests dominated by western red cedar and western hemlock — slower-growing giants usually found in high-rainfall habitats — are fully developed, self-perpetuating climax communities. The dry southeast coast of the island is striking in its divergence from the typical coniferous growth pattern. It is characterized by two broad-leaved species, the Garry oak and the Pacific madrona — shaggy, twisted trees that thrive in open parkland habitats with dry soils and mild winters.

Whatever the setting, the large trees provide a framework for many different forms of lesser vegetation, creating a rich spectrum of niches for the island's wildlife. All the varied associations of plants and animals now present on Vancouver Island have developed since the recession of the last ice age some 10,000 years ago. As the snowfalls diminished and the glaciers of the Vashon ice sheet retreated, life forms that had survived the 100,000-year deep-freeze — by migrating south — began to recolonize the island's naked surface. This process continues today. On a geological time-scale, the current phase of Vancouver Island's natural history is very recent, and still in a comparatively rapid stage of development.

Vancouver Island
March 1983

Tim Fitzharris

The Edge

DURING WINTER, rafts of scoters are found in sheltered bays and inlets along the island's coast. Here, often in association with other sea-birds, they forage for mussels, oysters, crabs, sea-urchins, and other marine animals. Smaller mollusks are ripped free of their moorings and swallowed whole. Given that some of these shells are tough enough to withstand the blow of a hammer, the strength of the avian gizzard that can grind them to tiny pieces is astonishing. In April, meandering strings of scoters wing northward to their nesting grounds. Some flocks follow the jagged coastline into northern British Columbia and Alaska, while others move cross-country into the Northwest Territories.

A white-winged scoter floats on the calm, fog-bound water of a secluded inlet.

A stretch of shoreline on the Juan de Fuca Straits. ▷

A small herd of curious northern sea-lions rises out of the surf.

THE NORTHERN SEA-LION may be awkward on land, but it moves through the cold Pacific Ocean with a powerful grace. Kept warm by thick blubber, its fusiform bulk is propelled by metre-long flippers to depths of over 150 metres. These animals swim in compact herds, feeding on squid, octopus, and a variety of coarse fish, as well as mollusks and crustaceans. The digestive tract required to process this varied fare is almost as long as a football field. Although their strength discourages predation by other carnivores, sea-lions must always be alert to the possibility of attack by killer whales and large sharks. In the past, many were shot by fishermen under the mistaken belief that they took a toll of commercial fish stocks.

When bickering sea-lions congregate on a rocky islet, their deep-throated bellows are easily heard above the roar of the surf. Mature bulls weighing a tonne or more dominate the haulouts (dry land rest areas) and rookeries (breeding areas). During the breeding season (June to July), each gathers a harem of ten to twenty cows, forsaking food completely for the more pressing business of reproduction. Occasionally, a cow — more agile and quick than the cumbersome bull — may slip from harem to harem to increase her chances of conceiving. If she succeeds, a single pup will be born the following spring.

Winter sunshine highlights the sleek but powerful form of a ▷ sea-lion.

THE KILLER WHALE is an awesome creature. A large bull can power its five muscular tonnes out of the water in a single vertical launch, or breach, that sees the tail flukes clear the waves by several metres. Its dorsal fin stands taller than a man, and overall length may reach nine metres. Surprisingly nimble for all their great size and strength, some killer whales have been observed playfully dunking terrified sea-birds by grabbing their dangling feet from below. Feeding behaviour, on the other hand, is no game — a whale surfacing with a sea-lion in its jaws will proceed to shake and bite its victim to pieces. Bold, rapacious, and skilful hunters, members of a pod often work co-operatively. While knowledge of their diet is incomplete, feeding habits appear to vary with location. For the orcas of the inner straits, the main summer food seems to be salmon. Certainly warm-blooded animals are important prey for all killer whales — the contents of one stomach included the remains of thirteen porpoises and fourteen seals.

Vancouver Island may well be the best place in the world to observe wild killer whales. The total offshore population is estimated at around 300. In addition to the spectacular breaching, their large repertoire of surface activities includes spy-hopping (rising vertically out of the water to look around), speed-swimming, tail-lobbing, and the dorsal fin slap. In Johnstone Strait, on the northeast coast of the island, the whales engage in another intriguing activity known as 'beach-rubbing'. Gathering near a short stretch of pebble beach, the members of a pod will spread out along the shore in order to rub themselves on the smooth stones, often with their bodies well out of the water. The reason for this behaviour is not known, but the whales appear to enjoy it. Human access to the region is now restricted by the British Columbia government, to protect the whales and this unique area from excessive disturbance.

A killer whale surfaces in the fading twilight of Johnstone Strait.

FOR THE BIRD-WATCHER, Vancouver Island is one of the most exciting areas in Canada. Not only does it offer a range of habitats from alpine to coastal, and semi-arid parkland to temperate rain forest, but it is also strategically located on the Pacific flyway. The surrounding marine environments support a varied abundance of pelagic and other wet-habitat species that land-locked bird-lovers cannot enjoy. Moreover, the mild winters attract many species from the harsher climates of the north and the interior, allowing birders in Victoria to register one of the highest counts in Canada (approximately 125 species) at the annual Christmas bird census.

APPEARING ALONG the island's coast during migration, the common tern is easily identified by its strong, thrusting flight and distinctive feeding behaviour. It hovers over the calm sea and plunges precipitously into the water, sometimes disappearing for several seconds before emerging with a small fish. Autumn migrants are often accompanied by parasitic jaegers: large, hawk-like birds that harrass the terns in order to steal their catch. The black-tipped bill of the adult is a sure way of distinguishing the common tern from the almost identical Arctic species.

Common terns rest on a kelp-strewn beach at low tide.

THE BIG-HEADED belted kingfisher is common in coastal lagoons and estuaries, and even along inland freshwater systems. It hunts with great flair, plummeting headlong into the water to seize a fish or crab passing unknowingly below the surface. Reappearing with a catch that is sometimes very nearly its own size, the kingfisher tears free of the water and, with tremendous effort, lifts its burden to the perch. But the battle is not over yet. The prey is bludgeoned against the snag and methodically minced from head to tail with the heavy beak. Only then, when all life has departed, does the hunter swallow its meal — head first.

A belted kingfisher rasps a staccato warning from its hunting perch.

Wing display is part of the courtship ritual of the male common goldeneye.

THE VIBRANT WHISTLING of the common goldeneye's wings carries a considerable distance. These ducks are exceedingly strong and swift fliers — some have been timed at over eighty kilometres per hour. Migrating in small flocks at high altitudes, goldeneyes from the forested inland regions winter along the coast. On the wintering grounds, the drakes engage in a spectacular courtship display, part of which involves doubling the head and neck backward almost to the tail, and simultaneously kicking up a great spray of water. The goldeneye is one of the few ducks that nest in holes in trees.

THE RED-BREASTED MERGANSER commonly winters along the island's beaches, estuaries, and lagoons. Its scientific name (*Mergus serrator*) alludes to the serrated, or saw-like, bill that assists the bird in grasping its slippery favourite food — fish. Often several of these ducks will string out abreast to drive small fish into the shallows where they are most easily caught. The drake is strikingly different from the female, with a shaggy metallic-green head and rich red-brown breast.

A female red-breasted merganser plows through the water in ▷ *pursuit of a fish.*

The tranquil water of a tidal pool is broken by a hungry great blue heron.

ONE OF THE SMALLEST American gulls, the Bonaparte's gull is another spring and fall migrant that visits the island's shores in large numbers. Early fall arrivals appear in August with their black-headed breeding plumage still in evidence. At this time of year they feed on small herring and sand lance that have been driven to the surface by hungry coho salmon. Local sport fishermen take advantage of this habit to locate good fishing sites.

◁ *Its reflection shimmering in the still water, a Bonaparte's gull preens.*

THE BEST-KNOWN and most widely distributed of all North American herons, the great blue heron finds the rich aquatic habitats and mild winters of the west coast particularly to its liking. More than one metre tall, with a wingspan of over two metres, it is a majestic animal, whether poised rock-still beside a tidewater pool or flying to a tree-top perch, broad wings pumping in slow motion and reed-like legs trailing behind. Although obviously adapted for feeding in shallow waters, the lanky heron is also at home in the trees, where it builds its large nest of woven branches and twigs.

SURROUNDING VANCOUVER ISLAND is a sliver of habitat as rich and varied as any on earth — the intertidal zone. The island's edge is doused, usually twice a day, by tidal waters so rich that a single litre may be clouded with 60 million microscopic plants and animals of more than 3,000 varieties. This conglomeration of tiny drifting forms is called plankton, and it represents the greatest mass of life on our planet. Many higher animals crowd the shoreline to feast on the riches that the tides bring.

The animal life along the edge varies not only with the substratum itself, which may be mud-flat, sandy beach, or jagged rock, but also with the amount of time that it is exposed to the air each day. Creatures at the high-tide line must be able to survive with only the occasional splash or spray of sea water, while those further down the beach are adapted to a life-style that is almost totally aquatic. The many different niches thus created are inhabited by a wide assortment of swimmers, crawlers, burrowers, and sitters. Most of the intertidal animals fall into two major categories — mollusks (including clams, mussels, oysters, and snails) and crustaceans (including crabs, shrimps, and barnacles).

JAGGED, ROCKY SHORELINE dominates the coastal areas of Vancouver Island, and sand or pebble beaches are rare. Fortunately, this habitat is ideal for many marine creatures. The waves breaking over these craggy surfaces assure an abundant supply of dissolved oxygen. For small animals, the shore offers shelter from predators and the pounding ocean surf. Innumerable cracks and fissures provide safe points of attachment for mussels, barnacles, chitons, limpets, sponges, crabs, sea-stars, snails, anemones, and urchins.

Various species of large kelp anchor themselves to these rocks. At high tide, those supported by air bladders are able to float free of the abrasive rock bed; at low tide, they become draped over the rocks in heavy mats, providing a moist refuge for animals that would otherwise perish from exposure to the drying effects of sun and wind.

Stranded at low tide, purple sea-stars as large as dinner plates seek cover in the rock-clinging kelp.

The habitat of the colourful blood star ranges from the intertidal zone to offshore depths of 650 metres.

Strands of matted kelp are outlined with a rare touch of frost.▷

AMONG THE MOST beautiful animals found in the rocky, kelp-draped tide pools are the various species of sea-stars, or starfish. Their brilliant colours and handsome patterns are marvels of natural design. Nevertheless, to many of the creatures that share its habitat — especially the clams and mussels — the blind, toothless, slow-moving sea-star is a fearsome and relentless predator. First, the arms, lined with hundreds of tiny suction cups, slowly spread the protective shell of the mollusk. Then, with grotesque efficiency, the sea-star extrudes its sac-like stomach through its mouth and into the vulnerable innards of its victim, digesting the meal on the spot.

Clusters of blue mussels anchor themselves to rocks and to each other by secreting silky threads that harden on contact with water or air. The bivalve shells of these mollusks are gently rounded and knife-edged on one side to resist wave action. Water enters and exits the open shell through two siphons, while planktonic organisms are filtered out by the gills. However, the filtration process is indiscriminate — many shellfish are poisoned by water polluted with petrochemicals, industrial and agricultural wastes, and even natural sea toxins such as red tide. Mollusks are instrumental components of the process by which the abundant plankton of the world's oceans is synthesized into a form that can be exploited by higher animals, including man.

◁ Blue mussels pile atop one another in a choice intertidal location.

Barnacles are crustaceans, and early in life they are quite similar in appearance to their relatives, the crabs and shrimps. However, after a period of growth, the larva fastens onto some hard surface — a rock, boat hull, or whale — never to move again. Lying on its back, it secretes a limey substance that forms a rock-hard multi-plated shell. When the tide is out, the plates slide together, creating a comfortable watertight fortress for the animal within. With the return of the sea, the upper hatch opens and the barnacle's legs, now modified into feather-like sweepers, extend into the swirl of plankton to gather food. More than twenty species of barnacles inhabit the waters around Vancouver Island. Some are pelagic, living on logs that drift with the currents of the north Pacific Ocean. The only time we catch a glimpse of these barnacles is when storms wash them onto the beaches.

A granular hermit crab cautiously emerges from an appropriated snail shell.

THE HERMIT CRAB is an active and entertaining representative of the intertidal life zone. Lacking an outer skeleton to cover the abdominal portion of its body, it carts around an abandoned snail shell for protection. Bolstered by this refinement in physique, it scavenges the bottom for dead organic matter, and battles readily (sometimes fatally) with any other hermits that cross its path. The large armoured pincers that are its chief weapons are also used to convey food to the mouth-parts. When the time comes for the growing hermit to take up larger quarters, the normally scrappy crustacean makes a hesitant exit from its shell and scuttles about in an agitated state until its tender rear is again safely encased.

FOUR-FIFTHS OF all the earth's animal species, including crabs, are protected by a tough outer shell, or exoskeleton. The various pieces of this armour are held together by an intricate series of sockets and hinges that allow movement, and, for the most part, the arrangement works very well. The only problem is that a young crab outgrows its rigid case two or three times a year. When this happens, the old shell splits and pops open, and the animal emerges looking pretty much the same as it did before. However, its new covering is very soft. To gain some growing room, the crab pumps itself up with water, releasing it only when the expanded shell has hardened once again. Species along the Vancouver Island coast range in size from 0.30 to 30.0 centimetres.

As scavengers, crabs fulfil an important function in cleaning up dead plant and animal matter that collects on the beaches. In turn, they are eaten by all manner of predators, especially octopus, rockfish, and sculpin.

After a few seconds of digging, only the eyes of this green shore crab will be visible above the mud.

THE SWIRL of planktonic life that abounds in the inshore waters affords many creatures the luxury of a largely sedentary existence. Among them is the sea anemone. It simply parks its tubular body in some tide-washed locale and extends its whorled tentacles — often of beautiful colour and configuration — into the soup to sample whatever happens by: small fish, worms, snails, shrimps, assorted marine larvae, even dead organic matter. This graceful, seemingly delicate shore-dweller can chew up and swallow a crab and spit out the left-overs in less than fifteen minutes. When exposed by an ebbing tide, the anemone shrinks into a dark, wrinkled stump.

Aggregate anemones feed amid a jumble of crab and limpet shells.

A river otter munches the tough shell of a rock crab.

THE RIVER OTTER is a regular hunter in the tide pools and shallow waters of the coast. Distinctive trails, bank burrows, and droppings laced with fish and crustaceans are evidence of its presence. The otter has several amphibious adaptations: a streamlined torso, short, powerful legs, webbed toes, and dense, waterproof fur. It pursues its underwater prey with an undulating, almost serpentine swimming motion. Smaller animals are eaten while the otter floats on its back in the water, but a large fish or crab will be ferried back to shore to be devoured behind a shelter of rock or driftwood. Even though it is not often seen, the otter is one of the most abundant mammals on Vancouver Island's coastline and offshore archipelagos.

Harbour seals forage in the shallows at high tide.

HARBOUR SEALS generally frequent the shallow waters close to shore, riding the high tide into bays and inlets to feed on inshore fish, crabs, and shrimps. Small family groups haul out on rocky islets and sometimes even log booms, awkwardly worming their way to a spot that will allow quick re-entry into the water. Unlike sea-lions, they do not gather into harems for reproductive purposes, though several females may seek out the same reef or sand-bar to give birth. The single pup, born in late May or June, suckles from its mother while she floats on her back in the water. Harbour seals become confident in protected environments, and it is not uncommon to see them mooching around Victoria's bustling downtown harbour.

True seals differ from sea-lions in that they have no external ears, and their front flippers are much smaller. Thus, while the sea-lion uses mainly its front flippers for propulsion in the water, the seal must rely on its hind limbs alone. On land, the sea-lion is supported by both pairs of flippers and can shuffle along fairly easily, whereas the seal can only wriggle ungracefully about on its belly.

Sea water regularly floods the rich intertidal zone of the rocky coast. ▷

A black oystercatcher transports a mussel into shallow water, where it will be easier to consume.

FOUND ONLY along the Pacific coast of North America, the black oystercatcher is an uncommon and exciting attraction even for local bird-watchers. Its crow-sized black body, pink legs, flattened scarlet bill, and bulging yellow eyes conspire to produce an almost clownlike appearance, and the effect is heightened when the bird takes to the air in a careening flight often accompanied by a wild, whooping call. Feeding primarily on crabs and limpets of the intertidal zone, the oystercatcher uses its sturdy laterally compressed bill to sever the mollusk's adductor muscle and free the juicy meat within. It lays its spotted, buff-coloured eggs in the hollows of a rocky islet or along the upper beach during May and June.

Tufted puffins nest in a handful of known colonies along Vancouver Island's coast.

AN AERIAL VIEW of Vancouver Island would show the surrounding waters dappled and dotted with hundreds of smaller islands. Of these, only a few offer the conditions necessary for reproduction by colonial nesting sea-birds. First, a major rookery must be remote enough to be free from predators, such as rats or mink, that might threaten reproductive activities. Second, an abundant food supply is essential. Thus the most prolific colonies are usually found in waters with strong currents which stir up nutrients from the bottom, in the process fertilizing the plankton that grows in the oxygenated water near the surface. The resulting abundance of plankton supports many fish, which in turn become a ready food source for sea-birds.

Individual sea-bird species are highly specialized in the type of terrain they can use for nesting. The tufted puffin requires an island with a bit of soil and turf, since it must excavate an underground burrow in which to cache its eggs. The rhinocerous auklet is similarly restricted, but it also needs a few shrubs or trees nearby, to cushion its customary after-dark, out-of-control crash landings. The pelagic cormorant, on the other hand, has trouble taking off. Therefore it prefers to nest on an island with precipitous cliffs that facilitate getting airborne. As the list of requirements expands, the number of islands that meet the criteria shrinks accordingly. The rare handful that remain are coveted pieces of real estate — crowded, brawling, odoriferous, and unique nuggets of natural history.

THE DOUBLE-CRESTED CORMORANT is not the kind of bird that immediately endears itself to humans. It has a grim, hawk-like visage, dark, greasy plumage, and a sickly, croaking call; it feeds its young by regurgitating partially digested fish; its breeding rookeries — nests, eggs, young, and adult birds alike — are plastered with its own haphazard droppings. But for all our aesthetic reservations, the cormorant is beautifully adapted to a coastal environment. A large, heavy-bodied bird almost a metre long, it is an expert fisher, able to adjust its own specific gravity to facilitate underwater pursuit of prey. Although derided for its laborious take-off and clumsy-looking flight, the cormorant can also commute rapidly between the fishing grounds and its cliff-side nesting colonies — flight speed has been timed at eighty kilometres per hour.

◁ *A glaucous-winged gull raids the nest of a double-crested cormorant.*

In the cold waters of Georgia Strait, a double-crested cormorant prepares to swallow a freshly caught fish.

THE GLAUCOUS-WINGED GULL is one of the most conspicuous birds both on Vancouver Island and along the entire British Columbia coast. A capable fisher at sea, it also scavenges along the beaches, docks, and dumps for garbage and dead animals that have been carried ashore. At low tide, it gathers mollusks, carries them aloft, and then drops them onto the rocks below to shatter the shells. These birds usually reproduce in colonies, building their nests of grasses, seaweed, marine debris, and a few feathers among the tufted hummocks of a small island.

THE PIGEON GUILLEMOT is a member of a group of diving sea-birds (including auks, auklets, murres, murrelets, and puffins) known as alcids. Most of them prefer the open sea, and come ashore only to nest. Pigeon guillemots resemble miniature penguins. Their plumage is mainly black and white, and they use their pointed wings to fly — quite literally — underwater, their webbed feet acting as rudders. The alcids' amazing skill in the water seems to have detracted somewhat from their aerial manoeuvres, however. A puffin may be caught simply by swinging a fish-landing net into its flight path — the feathered projectile is incapable of swerving in time to avoid capture.

This two-year-old glaucous-winged gull will soon acquire its snowy breeding plumage.

From a cliff edge overlooking the sea, a pigeon guillemot utters a faint piping whistle. ▷

Tiny offshore islands such as these abound along the outer coastline.

THE WESTERN EDGE of Vancouver Island is made up of rocky islets off-shore and a rugged stretch of coastline, largely uninhabited, slashed by broad fiords. An exception is the Long Beach area — a rare, sweeping expanse of sand and pounding surf that is part of the Pacific Rim National Park system. Including, to the south, the Broken Group Islands of Barkley Sound and the West Coast Trail, the park region is a haven for wildlife and a delight to the naturalist. In addition to bald eagles, migratory shore-birds and gray whales, sea-lions, tufted puffins, and Brandt's cormorants, it offers a wide variety of habitats to study and explore: coastal forest, sand dunes, bogs, mud-flats, sea-bird islands, streams, and tidal zones.

Northern elephant seals are often spotted off the west coast of Vancouver Island. More than six metres long, a large bull may weigh as much as three and a half tonnes.

EXCEPT DURING the winter months, the osprey is a fairly common sight along the seacoast and inland watercourses. It is a bird of regal appearance and exciting behaviour, preying almost entirely on fish snatched from the water with its powerful talons. The osprey's feet are even more specialized than those of other hawks. Spicules on the lower surfaces of the toes provide a firm grip on slippery prey, while the reversible outer toe permits the bird to strike with its talons symmetrically arranged (two forward, two backward), which prevents the fish from twisting free. The osprey generally spends a lot of time perched on dead shoreline snags. Once a fish is spotted, the bird will fly out over its victim, hover for a few seconds, and then make a steep dive, talons and beak foremost, shattering the water's surface with a spectacular momentum that often carries it completely from view.

◁ *Pelagic cormorants stand sentinel at a crowded cliff-edge nesting site.*

Rising above the water with its slippery prey gripped in both ▷ feet, an osprey carries a fish with the head pointed forward, to reduce wind resistance.

Forest and Woodland

Steller's jay

Illuminated by a rare shaft of sunlight, moss-wrapped hemlocks opportunistically straddle the fecund rotting trunk of a fallen giant.

RAIN FORESTS GROW in areas of abundant precipitation, and the conditions on Vancouver Island are ideal. Blowing in from the warm Pacific, the moisture-laden prevailing winds collide with the rising landscape and drench the forests below in up to four metres of water each year. The climax forests that thrive under these circumstances are dominated by western red cedar, western hemlock, and Sitka spruce. Mosses, ferns, and lichens carpet the soaring trunks, drape the branches, and cushion the forest floor. Here and there, the eerie gloom of the under-storey is cluttered with deadfalls and scattered clumps of salal, salmonberry, and Oregon grape, but on the whole it is surprisingly open, since the dense canopy prevents all but the most shade-tolerant species from growing.

Away from the coastal lowlands, much of what may be considered rain forest consists of that celebrated giant, the Douglas fir. Monumental as these stands may appear, they are nevertheless only temporary, sub-climax communities, for Douglas fir seedlings cannot grow in the shade of the parent trees. After about ten centuries of growth, the mature specimens begin to weaken, and eventually they topple over, to be replaced by hemlocks and cedars which require less light. Fortunately, since the recession of the last ice age 10,000 years ago, extensive fires have opened up the landscape fairly regularly, allowing for continued re-establishment of the Douglas fir forests that are widespread today.

IT IS IN the rain forests of the Pacific coast that the Douglas fir attains its most spectacular dimensions. Although a century of logging has destroyed most of the virgin stands, there are still a few groves on Vancouver Island in which the massive firs tower some thirty storeys into the fog and mist. A few colossal specimens are more than 1,000 years old. With a trunk diameter exceeding four metres, each is spacious enough to hold a pair of compact cars parked side by side. The bark alone, which sheathes the trunk in great rounded ridges, may be more than a foot thick.

Not many people would be able to put their arms around even the smaller trees (western hemlocks) in this Douglas fir rain forest at Cathedral Grove.

The dainty bell-shaped flowers of the salal shrub are only about one centimetre long.

The blossoms of the salmonberry shrub develop into raspberry-like fruit.

ABUNDANT SALAL and salmonberry shrubs are characteristic of the coniferous west coast forest, and rarely occur east of the Cascade Range. Salal, noted for its glossy, robust evergreen foliage, grows near the sea in dense, wind-sculptured hedges that are nearly impenetrable. Hikers who stray from established trails may also find themselves stonewalled by salmonberry shrubs, armed with stiff prickles. Appearing in February, the fragile rose-coloured blossoms of the salmonberry are especially radiant against the drab greens and browns of lingering winter.

LAND SNAILS are at home in the moist, shaded rain forest. Most active after dark, they feed on both dead and living vegetation of the forest floor. Cruising along on the soft, rippling, mucous-lubricated flesh of a large muscular foot, the snail glides over the foliage while its burred tongue rasps off the delicate cells of a plant stem or mows through a crop of algae. More visible in daytime are the snails' relatives, the large slugs. Appearing in various colours and patterns, some of them grow to lengths of twelve centimetres or more.

Stalked eyes and feelers enable this land snail to scout the path ahead.

THE RED SQUIRREL is Vancouver Island's only native squirrel. One of the marten's main sources of nutrition, it is an important link in the forest food chain. This master of arboreal acrobatics is able to leap three metres from branch to branch and scamper about the twisted pathways every which way — even upside-down. Such dare-devilry is not as reckless as it may seem, however: red squirrels have been known to survive falls of more than ten storeys without injury.

THE MARTEN is a typical denizen of the island's coniferous forests, avoiding burned-over, logged, or sub-climax habitats. Although adapted to arboreal travel, it also spends considerable time on the forest floor, bounding through the ample debris and close vegetation. The objects of these largely nocturnal rambles are the mice and voles that account for about two-thirds of its dietary intake. Martens have an insatiable curiosity, and have been known to trace an enticing scent into a campsite or wilderness cabin. This forthright inquisitiveness makes them easy victims to all kinds of traps, and tens of thousands are lost to the fur trade each year.

A red squirrel nibbles on rosehips softened and blackened by a winter of aging.

Beady eyes shining brightly, a marten pauses momentarily at ▷ a forest deadfall.

THE COUGAR POPULATION of Vancouver Island is one of the most dense in the world. Almost everything about this big cat is designed for efficient killing: keen senses, a lithe, graceful body, large canine teeth, and well-armed, club-like paws. Yet these formidable attributes do no more than allow the cougar to maintain a population level that is in fact limited by the health and abundance of its prey. Columbian black-tailed deer comprise almost eighty per cent of its diet. The cougar is primarily nocturnal, prowling noiselessly among the shadows and manoeuvring stealthily into position for sudden attack. Springing onto the deer's back, it bites deeply into the neck and rakes the head and neck with its claws. In most cases, the victim collapses under the terrible onslaught, goes into shock, and dies quickly. The cat then drags its kill to a secluded eating spot.

◁ *Alert but unafraid, a buck Columbian blacktail stands motion-less in the forest under-storey.*

A cougar peers cautiously through the drooping limbs of a ▷
western red cedar.

THE NORTHWESTERN GARTER SNAKE roams a variety of habitats, and may just as often be sighted weaving through a grassy meadow as hunting the waters of a tidal pool. Prowling for frogs, fish, slugs, small birds, and mice, the serpent seizes its quarry with a forward lunge of the head. When the initial struggle subsides, it slowly works its elastic jaws around its victim; needle-like teeth angled rearward keep the body moving steadily toward the powerful digestive tunnel. Once the prey is swallowed, the snake retreats to some secluded location to sleep off its apparent over-indulgence. The heavy overlapping scales of the garter snake's belly are equipped with a complex system of muscles that allows each plate to thrust separately against the terrain. Repeated many times in succession, this movement produces the fluid beauty of serpentine locomotion.

THE METALLICALLY HUED Pacific tree-frog is found from sea-level to alpine regions throughout Vancouver Island. Small size — the slender body is only two to four centimetres long — and adhesive toe-pads combine to give this agile amphibian little appreciation of gravitational force. It clambers and vaults about the shrubbery, and even ventures high into the tree-tops in search of insects. Generally secretive, the tree-frog can sit motionless for long periods, waiting for prey to draw near enough to be snagged in a single outflinging of its long sticky tongue. Reproduction takes place in small ponds and backwaters.

Aided by sticky toe-pads, a Pacific tree-frog clings to an ▷
unopened bud.

ALWAYS SHY and evasive of humans, spiders operate in an exquisite microworld. The young, perfectly developed when they emerge from the egg sac, immediately lay down a silken drag-line which anchors them to the substratum wherever they travel. The silk is ejected as a liquid from organs known as spinnerets; on contact with air it hardens into a material stronger than steel, in some cases only half a millionth of a centimetre thick, and virtually invisible.

DISTINCTIVE MARKINGS and unusual tail-like projections on its hind wings make the western tiger swallowtail one of the best-known butter-flies on Vancouver Island. Most often seen in flight as it sails through the woodlands in search of nectar, like other swallowtails it may also be observed drawing moisture from wet soil or puddles. The brilliant green caterpillars of this species feed on various members of the willow family.

◁ *Since its eyesight is poor, the orb-weaver spider relies on changes in thread tension and vibration to locate victims snared in its web.*

A western tiger swallowtail spreads its wings to absorb needed warmth from the early morning sunlight.

The advent of the rainy season in fall brings a proliferation of ▷
varied and colourful fungi on the forest floor. Here questiona-
ble stropharius grows among fallen madrona berries.

The golden chanterelle is one of the most delicious mushrooms
anywhere. Cap diameter ranges from three to ten centimetres.

A SUBSPECIES of the widely distributed black-tailed deer, the coast deer, or Columbian black-tail, is distinguished from the inland race by its small antlers and the absence of the usual white rump patch. Bands of these deer roam the humid western slopes of the Coast Range and the off-shore islands, some migrating to the mountain-tops and high valleys in summer to feed on alpine vegetation. Fortunately, they also have a con-venient appetite for the Douglas fir, salal, and western red cedar available in winter, when they return to the lower ranges to take shelter in the coniferous forests. Well-adapted to coastal life, blacktails will often strike out across the straits to reach an island that may offer better forage.

SAW-WHET OWLS are so tolerant of humans that more than one has been stalked to its roost and caught in the hand. Only eighteen centi-metres long, these small nocturnal predators feed mainly on shrews and deer mice.

All owls are renowned for their keen eyesight, but their sense of hearing is just as remarkable. The feathered facial disks surrounding the eyes work acoustically, funnelling sounds to the ear openings on either side of the head. In many species, these openings differ from one another in size and shape, permitting the owl to track moving prey with great accuracy by means of triangulation. Experiments have shown that some species are capable of hunting by sound alone.

◁ *Cached in the forest under-storey while its mother browses for food, a blacktail fawn directs a large ear toward possible danger.*

A saw-whet owl uses its wing to 'mantle' the small bird it has just captured. This behaviour is apparently intended to conceal the catch and thereby prevent theft by larger birds.

The band-tailed pigeon swoops down to its feeding ground like a striking hawk, only to flutter about the shrubbery in search of nuts and berries.

Ripening late in the year, the fruit of the cascara buckthorn ▷
is relished by numerous birds.

AUTUMN ON Vancouver Island is a season of subtle change. In the south, light rains and an increase in the frequency of cloudy days mark the end of the dry summer. The common deciduous trees — red alder, black cottonwood, and bigleaf maple — shift colour almost imperceptibly. Though even at their peak they show only a tawny yellow pigmentation, it is nevertheless quite brilliant in the heavy coniferous setting. The cascara buckthorn is a colourful exception, its foliage intermittently daubing the forests with a rich crimson hue.

The band-tailed pigeon is one of the many species that feast on the island's wild harvest before migrating south. Although it is primarily a bird of the American southwest, its range slivers northward along the coast to include Vancouver Island.

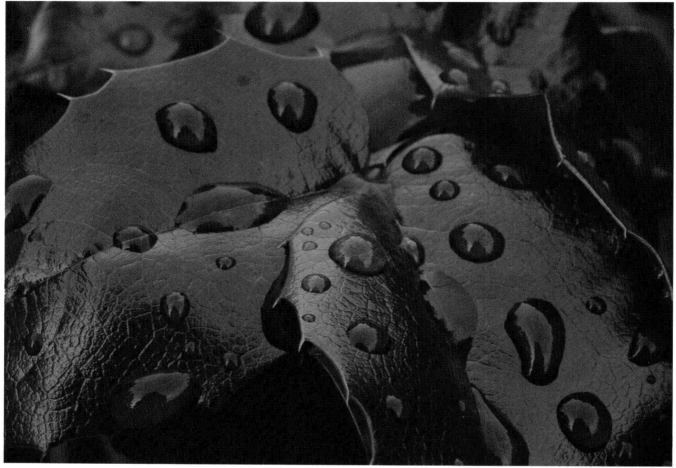

Winter raindrops collect on the leaves of tall Oregon grape.

The impressive antennae of the male Polyphemus moth can ▷ detect the presence of a female several kilometres away.

OREGON GRAPE is noted for its leathery-textured, spike-edged leaves, which shine as if they were wet. Remaining on the shrub for two or three years, they acquire metallic tints of bronze, orange, and vermilion before they drop. The lemon-yellow flowers are delicately perfumed, and produce clusters of dark blue berries softly dusted with a pale powdery bloom. Cooked and sweetened, the fruit yields a delicious jelly. Tall Oregon grape (*Berberis aquifolium*) commonly grows in open sunny locations, while a similar but smaller species (*B. nervosa*) has a low, spreading growth pattern that covers the ground in deeply shaded coniferous forests.

VANCOUVER ISLAND is isolated from the rest of the continent not only by water but also by a formidable mountain wall — the Coast and Cascade Ranges of the adjacent mainland. As a result, many plants and animals commonly dispersed over the continent are missing entirely, while others appear only in a modified Vancouver Island version. For example, the black-capped chickadee, cherished by bird-lovers from St John's to Vancouver, has never extended its range the few extra kilometres across the Strait of Georgia. Fortunately, its absence is redressed by the presence of the chestnut-backed chickadee, a distinct species with many of the same endearing attributes. In general, the mountains have kept in more birds than they have kept out. The glaucous-winged gull and pelagic cormorant are two examples of species that, in Canada, are restricted to the west coast.

Terrestrial mammals are a different case. Vancouver Island has not a single coyote, chipmunk, moose, caribou, mountain sheep, mountain goat, bobcat, lynx, hare, ground squirrel, mole, gopher, lemming, porcupine, grizzly bear, or fisher — to list only some of the more prominent omissions. However, it does boast one of the rarest mammals in the world — the Vancouver Island marmot. Wholly confined to the island, its total population is estimated by some biologists at fewer than three hundred animals. Many native mammals, including the elk, wolf, shrew, and black-tailed deer, exhibit characteristics that betray their isolation from kindred species east of the mountains.

THE BLACK BEARS of Vancouver Island are unusually large, and lack the brown and cinnamon colour phases of bears on the mainland. Brutish, cantankerous creatures, they venture into the alpine country in summer to graze in the lush meadows. Although plants and carrion comprise ninety per cent of their diet, they will take young elk, black-tailed deer, marmots, mice, or voles whenever an easy opportunity arises. For all its lumbering bulk (a large male may weigh as much as two or three refrigerators), the black bear can generate surprising speed when pressed. Bouncing over the terrain like some huge furry ball, the rugged bruin will plunge unhesitatingly into a swollen, ice-choked river if its destination lies on the other side.

◁ *The coastal forest is home to the sprightly chestnut-backed chickadee.*

Scarred from past battles, a black bear advances through ▷
the brush.

Bigleaf maples and licorice ferns glisten after a brief shower.

Every spring, the forests of southern Vancouver Island are brightened by the showy blooms of the Pacific dogwood, British Columbia's floral emblem.

THE WOLF: a cruel, bony, drooling beast that eats grandmothers. Until recently, such was the popular but hardly accurate view of this graceful, intelligent carnivore. Indeed, wolf society exhibits elements of organization, co-operation, and shared responsibility seldom seen in the animal world. The young are cared for by the entire pack. The male brings food to the nursing mother and later to the pups. Should the mother die, the father will take over their care, and

◁ *Wolves on Vancouver Island are generally smaller and darker than their mainland cousins. However, hybrid populations are growing as mainland wolves swimming the straits invade the island's eastern regions.*

if they are not yet weaned, another pack female may adopt them. Unmated aunts and uncles will guard and play with the pups while the parents are out hunting. Members of a pack often display mutual affection, romping, nuzzling, tail-wagging, and, occasionally, brawling. But wolves are meat-eaters. Unable to differentiate between natural prey and domesticated animals or wild species that man has earmarked for his personal killing pleasure, they are often victimized by indiscriminate campaigns of extermination. As a result of this ruthless approach to the problem, the wolf is one of the many large carnivores that are among the earth's most rapidly disappearing natural treasures.

THE PACIFIC MADRONA is Canada's only broad-leaved evergreen tree. It lends an almost tropical flavour to the island's southeast coast, blooming in February in sheltered locations near the sea. Its peeling lime-green and red trunk makes it conspicuous on rocky bluffs and other well-drained sunny sites. A large specimen may attain a height of twenty-five or thirty metres, and a diameter of one metre or more. The madrona's frequent associate, the Garry oak, is smaller and somewhat more common — a naked, gnarled and twisted form that accentuates the sombreness of the winter landscape. It produces acorns which are eaten by mice, squirrels, deer, and bears, as well as birds such as the Steller's jay, northwestern crow, and band-tailed pigeon. The Garry oak/Pacific madrona association is almost completely confined to Vancouver Island and the Gulf Islands, with only a few small groves on the British Columbia mainland.

A Pacific madrona glows evergreen against the backdrop of a January storm.

A clump of Garry oak is denuded by the approach of winter.

ALTHOUGH MOST of Vancouver Island is covered by coniferous coastal forest, a narrow strip of lowland on the eastern coast exhibits quite different vegetation. Extending from the southeast tip of the island northward along the Georgia Strait for 250 kilometres, this area is British Columbia's most westerly dry belt. It is shielded from the rain-laden Pacific winds by the Olympic and insular mountains, which deflect the air upward and cause it to release its moisture before it reaches the inner straits. Most of the precipitation (78 centimetres per year, about the same as the Toronto average) falls during the winter. This dry, sunny, almost Mediterranean climate produces a flora dominated by two tree species that one would normally expect to find further south — the Garry oak and the Pacific madrona. The open, park-like forests in which they grow are particularly renowned for their abundance of spring-flowering plants.

The rich magenta blooms of the satin-flower shimmer on their slender stalks in the slightest whisper of wind.

MOST OF THE PLANTS shown here begin to bloom in early March in the Garry oak/Pacific madrona habitats of southern Vancouver Island.

◁ *The dogwood's apparent 'petals' are really modified leaves surrounding clusters of small greenish-white flowers.*

They are only a small sample of the spectacular display of early spring wildflowers that brings just fame to the region. Indeed, local botany enthusiasts can list twenty-five or thirty wild plant species — some native, some introduced — that flower during the month of January alone.

The graceful, sweeping form of the white fawn-lily makes it one of Vancouver Island's best-known flowers. At the peak of the display, these huge nodding blooms are scattered throughout the forest.

BLOOMING IN APRIL or May on Vancouver Island, the calypso, or fairy-slipper, orchid is found in shaded stands of Douglas fir, grand fir, and other conifers. Its small white bulb is embedded in a layer of moss and needles, and only a single shiny green leaf grows at the base of the reddish stem. The floral parts of the delicately tinted blossom show remarkable evolutionary adaptation to ensure cross-pollination by insects. The lip, or slipper, serves as a landing platform for airborne visitors. When an insect alights, the tiny hairs and rich coloration guide it to the nectar and sexual parts of the interior flower.

Calypso orchids glow like jewels in the moist, shaded under-storey of a coniferous forest. ▷

Shooting stars are often found growing in moist open mead-ows. Even when the plant is not in flower, a ground-hugging rosette of thick smooth leaves is a sure identifying mark.

◁ *A bumble-bee forages among the clustered four-petalled flowers of wintercress, a stiff, upright plant growing to a height of sixty centimetres.*

*The dwarf monkey-flower — a tiny annual blossom only one ▷
centimetre across — is usually found in upland regions.*

*A honey-bee hovers above the beckoning inflorescence of
early camas, which blooms in April or May.*

THE RETURN of the tiny rufous hummingbird from its Mexican wintering grounds brightens the island's forests every spring. With dazzling speed and flashes of crimson iridescence, it jets about the clearings in search of small insects, spiders, and the nectar of early flowers. No bigger than the end segment of a human thumb (ten of them weigh less than a slice of bread), hummingbirds have the highest metabolic rate

◁ *Every year, the rufous hummingbird returns to the island just when the red-flowered currant is blooming.*

of any warm-blooded vertebrates, with the possible exception of shrews. They must feed almost continually, or face quick starvation. A human expending energy at the same rate would require the evaporation of about forty litres of perspiration per hour, merely to keep his skin temperature below the boiling point of water; he would have to eat roughly double his weight in hamburgers every day. When the weather cools unexpectedly or food is not available, the hummingbird conserves energy by lowering its metabolism to a state of dormancy.

THE MOUNTAINOUS TERRAIN of Vancouver Island is striated with hundreds of streams and small rivers that carry the high-country runoff and melting snowpack back to the sea. In addition, long, glacier-gouged lakes stretch like fingers through the mountains for miles, while many smaller pot-hole formations occur at the headwaters of rivers and streams. Young by geological standards (only about 10,000 years old), these cold, deep, rocky-bottomed lakes can support few fish other than cold-water species such as salmon and trout. In contrast, the lakes closer to sea-level are enriched by an accumulation of organic matter and other nutrients that encourages the growth of plankton, aquatic plants, and the ensuing retinue of grazers and predators: salamanders, snails, crayfish, dragonflies, waterfowl, muskrats, and raccoons, among many others.

Rocky, quick-flowing streams such as this are ideal sprawning grounds for salmon.

A sleepy raccoon rouses momentarily from its daytime rest in the crotch of a pine.

SINCE A RACCOON'S ideal habitat is a forested area near water, it's not surprising that the small, dark race found on Vancouver Island is widespread. The typical island raccoon spends the day asleep, if not in a den (a hollow log, a small cave, even a garbage can), then simply perched in a tree. Once the sun goes down, it wakes up and heads for the beach, perhaps sharpening its appetite on a frog, June beetle, or deer mouse before reaching the real feast waiting at the tideline. Aided by its keen nose and eyes, it uses sensitive fingers to search carefully among the smooth pebbles, in the tide pools, and under rocks for mollusks and crustaceans.

In November, coastal streams about the island are littered with the bodies of spent chum salmon.

FIVE SPECIES OF SALMON inhabit the coastal and interior waters of Vancouver Island: the chum, sockeye, pink, chinook, and coho. For all of them, life begins in the gravel bed of a freshwater stream. Newly hatched salmon, or alevins, are equipped with sac-like appendages that carry enough nourishment to support them through the first few days of life. When the sacs are used up, the fish — now known as fry — feed on insects and plankton for a few weeks to three years, depending on the species. Eventually heading downstream for salt water, they spend the next two to eight years foraging in the Pacific, often straying hundreds of miles from their birthplace. At maturity, the salmon abandon their far-flung odyssey and return, miraculously, to the very stream in which they once hatched. Now, at last, mating takes place. The eggs are laid in a hollow excavated by the female's tail, then fertilized externally by milky secretions from the male. This frenzied activity is the salmon's last, and their exhausted bodies are eaten by scavengers — bears, gulls, eagles, ravens, and crows, to name only a few.

◁ *Visible just below the surface of the water, a school of salmon gathers strength for the steep ascent ahead.*

Fallen bigleaf maple and red alder leaves will enrich the waters of this coastal stream. ▷

A red-tailed hawk pauses from plucking its recent kill (an American coot) to scrutinize the shoreline.

A tangle of red alder clings to the cedar-crowded shoreline of a small lake. This species grows rapidly, often establishing itself on new ground ahead of the conifers.

IN AN UNDISTURBED forest, the ground is strewn with a jumble of rotting trunks, dead branches, seeds, cones, berries, animal droppings, and fallen leaves and needles. Although it seems unlikely, the future beauty and well-being of the forest are vitally dependent on this mass of rubbish. When trees die or leaves fall, their molecules still contain the energy of stored sunlight. Thus they can nourish fungi, bacteria, slime moulds, and the many kinds of tiny animals that inhabit the forest floor. Small holes appearing in leaves, bark, and wood mark the beginning of the attack. Tunnelling ever deeper as they feed, snails, millipedes, earwigs, woodlice, and others gradually weaken the material's structure. Birds and mammals claw and chip at the wood to search out these grubs, accelerating the decomposition process. A leaf soon deteriorates to little more than a net of tough veins and a few clinging bits. Bacteria and other microscopic organisms continue to live on these sparse remains, breaking the material down to its elemental components. All the dead organic debris of the forest floor undergoes the same process of decay. Eventually, the litter's important elements — nitrate, sulfate, phosphate, calcium, and magnesium — are returned to the water in the soil. The cycle is completed when these nutrients are absorbed by roots, and once again serve a vital function in the cells of a living tree.

◁ *The rotting wood of these dead trees will nurture fungi and insects, which in turn will provide food for woodpeckers and swallows. Eventually, a trunk cavity may harbour a clutch of wood duck eggs or a brood of red squirrels.*

A female wood duck, delicately patterned in soft grey, remains alert while her mate preens.

THE DENSE, WATERPROOF fur of the muskrat is composed of a soft, air-trapping inner pelt and an outer layer of coarse guard hairs. The largest North American rat (the average male weighs about one kilogram), this amphibious rodent is capable of swimming 100 metres underwater and can remain submerged for up to seventeen minutes. It frequents the marshy borders of lakes and rivers, feeding on pondweeds, sedges, and other emergent vegetation. Muskrats live in family groups, either in water lodges constructed of thatched aquatic plants or in bank burrows. Their main predators on Vancouver Island are mink, wolves, eagles, and domestic dogs.

A female hooded merganser pinches the head of a fish before swallowing it. These diminutive ducks (the average wingspan is only 0.6 metres) nest in hollow trees.

Sitting on the edge of its lodge, a muskrat grooms its pelt. ▷

The Pacific madrona keeps its broad evergreen leaves throughout the winter.

◁ *Snow is rare in the island's southern agricultural regions, where the ring-necked pheasant finds suitable habitat in the hedgerows and brush.*

111

The Alpland

Alpine arnica

ABOVE VANCOUVER Island's chequer-board of forests and broad logging scars rise the treeless alpine regions. Fragile but relatively unspoiled habitats, the mountains extend over most of the island. Rarely exceeding 2,200 metres, the magnificent ice-crowned peaks of even the highest ranges are insignificant in comparison with the Coast or Rocky Mountain ranges. Nevertheless, their natural history includes many features characteristic of much greater heights.

On the island, alpine habitat appears at surprisingly low elevations — usually around 1,200 metres. Toiling climbers are invariably delighted when they emerge from the enveloping forest into this far-flung, open, rolling meadowland. Scattered clumps of yellow cedar, balsam fir, and mountain hemlock replace the common trees of lower elevations. In favourable areas, the usual patches of red and white heather merge into spreading carpets. As the trees diminish, the hillsides are claimed by lively splashes of alpine wildflowers. Lupines, lilies, paintbrushes, and daisies grow in frantic profusion, to make the most of the short growing season. Higher still, the soil thins, and the gnarled but enduring vegetation finally gives way to ice, torn rock, and jagged peaks.

THE VARIETY of wildlife that permanently resides above timber-line is limited by the harsh conditions. Assorted amphibians and invertebrates dwell in the still pools and small lakes. Ice-worms ply the snowpack while marmots sleep in their burrows below. The population swells in summer, however, when many different animals venture up to the meadows to feed on the alpine vegetation. The white-tailed ptarmigan is one of the few birds to breed in the alpine zone. It lays its splotchy, buff-coloured eggs on the rocky slopes, and later shepherds its chicks about the meadows in search of insects, seeds, berries, and flowers. Another species that breaks somewhat with normal practice is the blue grouse. After rearing its family in the logging slashes and natural clearings of lower elevations, it spends the winter feeding on the coniferous buds and needles of the timber-line ridges.

The blue grouse is a winter inhabitant of the coniferous mountain forests.

THE ELK of Vancouver Island are larger and darker than those on the Canadian mainland. Mature bulls further distinguish the race by developing antlers with terminal cups. Such differences have led scientists to class the island population as a distinct subspecies (*Cervus canadensis rooseveltii*), commonly known as Roosevelt elk. During the autumn rut, the stags are truculent, thrashing the bushes with their antlers, rolling in urine-soaked wallows, bugling, and sparring with intruding males. A dominant bull may succeed in gathering a harem of up to thirty hinds and calves.

A bull elk in rut is on the look-out for rival males.

A stand of young balsam firs sags under the weight of a fresh snowfall.

A VANCOUVER ISLAND winter would be hardly recognizable to Canadians living east of the Coast Range. On the exposed outer coast, it is a season of rain, heavy fog, and mists blown in from the sea, with temperatures hovering around +5 degrees centigrade. The rain forests luxuriate in such conditions, trembling only during periods of storm, when a gale ripping in from the ocean can snap off a spruce or cedar two metres in diameter. Along the more protected inner straits, the mild, wet winters replenish moisture lost during summer, paving the way for the resurgence of mosses, ferns, and fungi. At higher elevations away from the sea, winter takes on more typically Canadian proportions. Snow accumulates in the mountains, streams and lakes freeze over, and temperatures plummet. Marmots and black bears are forced into hibernation, while elk and deer retreat into the valleys, where foraging is easier in the lighter snows of wind-swept hillsides.

Chest-deep in the lushness of an alpine meadow, a Columbian ▷ black-tailed deer detects an alien presence.

Completely unafraid of man, the gray jay is a common sight in the forested mountain regions.

◁ *Elegant flowers of wild columbine project over a mountain stream.*

The pure colours of scarlet paintbrush, senecio, and broad-leaved lupine accentuate the vivid green of an alpine meadow. ▷

A skipper butterfly sips nectar from a mountain daisy.

The beautifully sculptured blooms of red mountain heather adorn the slopes and plateaux above timber-line.

A rare clump of smooth douglasia clings to the rim of an exposed terrace.

Perched on a rocky outcrop, a Vancouver Island marmot sniffs the pure air of its mountain domain. ▷

IN A RESTRICTED handful of the island's alpine regions lives one of the rarest creatures in North America — the Vancouver Island marmot. This chunky, burrow-dwelling rodent closely resembles the woodchuck. Playful and inquisitive, it romps over the talus debris of its home range without a thought for the precarious state of its existence. In April, the marmot tunnels out through the snow to forage on the sparse vegetation of rocky, precipitous hillsides. Later in the season, its diet includes Indian paintbrush, spreading phlox, tiger lilies, and huckleberries. Among the factors that may threaten the survival of this unique species are logging practices that deter populations from expanding to neighbouring mountain-tops, disturbance by skiers and hikers, and predation by all the large island carnivores, including man.

Glacier lily

Index of Plates

Selected References

Bandoni, R.J., and A.F. Szczawinski. *Guide to Common Mushrooms of British Columbia* (Handbook Series no. 24). Victoria: British Columbia Provincial Museum, 1964.

Banfield, A.W.F. *The Mammals of Canada.* Toronto: University of Toronto Press, 1974.

Bodsworth, Fred. *The Pacific Coast.* Toronto: Natural Science of Canada Ltd., 1970.

Carl, G. Clifford. *Amphibians of British Columbia* (Handbook Series no. 2). Victoria: British Columbia Provincial Museum, 1966.

—. *Guide to Marine Life of British Columbia* (Handbook Series no. 21). Victoria: British Columbia Provincial Museum, 1966.

—. *Reptiles of British Columbia* (Handbook Series no. 3). Victoria: British Columbia Provincial Museum, 1960.

—, W.S. Clemens, and C.C. Lindsey. *The Fresh-Water Fishes of British Columbia* (Handbook Series no. 5). Victoria: British Columbia Provincial Museum, 1948.

Clark, Lewis J., and John G. Trelawny, ed. *Wild Flowers of the Pacific Northwest: From Alaska to Northern California.* Sidney, B.C.: Gray's Publishing Ltd., 1976.

Cornwall, Ira E. *The Barnacles of British Columbia* (Handbook Series no. 7). Victoria: British Columbia Provincial Museum, 1955.

Hitchcock, C.L., and A. Cronquist. *Flora of the Pacific Northwest.* Seattle: University of Washington Press, 1973.

Johnson, M.E., and H.J. Snook. *Seashore Animals of the Pacific Coast.* New York: Dover Publications, 1967.

Kirk, Ruth. *Olympic Rain Forest.* Seattle: University of Washington Press, 1966.

Lyons, Chester P. *Trees, Shrubs and Flowers to Know in British Columbia.* Toronto: J.M. Dent & Sons (Canada) Ltd., 1965.

McTaggart-Cowan, Ian, and Charles J. Guiget. *The Mammals of British Columbia* (Handbook Series no. 11). Victoria: British Columbia Provincial Museum, 1956.

Ricketts, Edward F., and Jack Calvin. *Between Pacific Tides.* Stanford, Cal.: Stanford University Press, 1962.

Smith, Ian. *The Unknown Island.* Vancouver: Douglas & McIntyre Ltd., 1978.

Terres, John K. *The Audubon Society Encyclopedia of North American Birds.* New York: Alfred A. Knopf Inc., 1980.